D0761307

DEEP
POCKETS

SAINT JULIAN PRESS

POETRY

PRAISE for DEEP POCKETS

Early on in this fine collection, an old dog "plunges her snout deep in the sloppy pocket / of the sensual present." So it is that the deep pockets of Daniel Thomas are tongued and explored again and again in generous poems of love and of longing, of grief and of guilt. Thomas brings a precision of line and a vulnerability of feeling to convince us, finally, that "heaven / and despair touch like dew and fog." These are poems to keep and to ponder as we seek—each one of us— our own ways forward into this world.

Paul J. Willis, author of *Getting to Gardisky Lake*

Like the snow that falls through so many of his poems, Daniel Thomas's words create shapes that outline the essential form of the things we love: the beauty of nature, the bonds of familial love, the mystery of being alive. Incantatory cadences and wordplay harness our attention and leave us vulnerable, open to revelations about the things we once knew and had forgotten. This is a collection to savor and dwell within.

Gregory Wolfe, Editor, *Image*

Deep Pockets is a profound meditation on human relationship, organically integrating classical literary influences from Dostoevsky to Dante. "My charts and compass lead me inward," Daniel Thomas says in one poem; this interior search half-paradoxically leads to what he calls in another poem "the soul's mystery in the material world." As in the book's ambitious centerpiece, "Three Women," these elegant, meticulously crafted poems map the cardinal points of a generously rewarding world Thomas invites his readers to share and explore.

Thomas R. Smith, author of
The Foot of the Rainbow and *The Glory*

In *Deep Pockets,* Daniel Thomas carefully unpacks a heart's journey of decades. He does not hurry through; his eloquence is spelled by moments of speechlessness, a respect for the untellable. Yet, a story gets told, mysteries intact, concerning shades of love; longing in a marriage that endures; children who "…even in the quietest room / …listen to him with all their being / and one ear closed." A beloved son goes to war; parents grow old and slip away; he cuts himself adrift at middle age, to his own surprise, and ventures "from known to unknown." He travels, carrying with him the classics, invoking gods, fools and wanderers who made the journey before him. Like them, he seeks in the nether realms and questions God.

Thomas's poems carry the wisdom and grace of the Old World, exploring matters of faith and conscience in an age where tenets have lost their purchase. But the real gold to be mined from this volume lies in the poet's deep connection to—and unusual tenderness for—his father, whose grand presence and unthinkable absence bind the book together. Take *Deep Pockets* with you, let it be the book you save from fire, read it on your journey.

Enid Osborn, author of *When The Big Wind Comes* and
Poet Laureate of Santa Barbara, California 2017-2019

If I were to say that the underlying observation in *Deep Pockets* is that nothing is as it seems, you might sigh and turn away. . . another cliché. But wait: what if that were actually *true?* What if, despite millennia of philosophizing, we don't have any *a priori* knowledge of the world, apart from our arrival in it, as Thomas writes in "Birthing George?" What if—though mentally—we can draw abstract deductions from abstract propositions, we can only really live inductively, from phenomena to phenomena?

Frequently set within an Italian landscape, the genius of *Deep Pockets* is the precision with which it views this inductive world, as Thomas moves through love and children and age, effectively turning each in his hand and examining it as if it were a Borgesian antique vase in which, if you looked closely enough, you could see every depth of love and loss, though the result might be too overwhelming to translate into another medium.

In his haunting, eight-part sequence, "Three Women," Thomas considers his relationships with his daughter, his wife, his mother—and one more, difficult to identify, in a sense love itself. These are among the best commentaries on love I've read—and there are a lot of commentaries on love in poetry—in part because Thomas so precisely renders the scenes from which certain emotions arise, and the futility, at times, of saying anything more about them than what they themselves imply, which might even be contradictory and so a source of grief.

What people do, in Thomas's book, is—to borrow a title from Marie Howe—"what the living do," however mundane that may sound: just as it was not mundane for Howe in her remarkable book, it is not mundane for Thomas. The diurnal is a continuous surprise in *Deep Pockets*. We must simply, this wonderful book suggests, be brave enough to accept that.

Thomas Simmons, author of *Now* and
Bring Your Nights with You: New and Selected Poems, 1975-2015

DEEP POCKETS

Poems By

DANIEL THOMAS

SAINT JULIAN PRESS
HOUSTON

Published by
SAINT JULIAN PRESS, Inc.
2053 Cortlandt, Suite 200
Houston, Texas 77008

www.saintjulianpress.com

ISBN-13: 978-0-9986404-9-5
ISBN: 0-9986404-9-2
Library of Congress Control Number: 2018938189

Cover Photo: Alankaar Sharma
Author Photo: Jacqueline Pilar

This book is dedicated to

Ellie, Gabe, Jamie and George

CONTENTS

THREE WOMEN

DEEP
POCKETS

Painting the Clouds

ICE STORM

Tires spin. Snowflakes swirl in the light beams
between bumpers. A mess of cars stretch head
to tail, like buffalo blinded in a great plains blizzard.

I strike out in darkness, trudging over a hill.
On the city's border, airplanes hunch on runways.
Ice has glazed the world to fossils and artifacts.

I cross a moonlit village, where a man chops a shelter
out of ice, another shivers sewing a fur coat
with sinews, a woman eats raw fish beside a futile fire.

The power plants have crumbled. The satellites are dark.
All the birds have flown this startling silence.
What's left is only the life inside us.

ADDICTION

Fade up on a black jacket sprawled
among broken bottles. To get the story going,
he cuts the shot short. He remembers mornings

when gin bottles crowded his bed, and his hands
shook until the movie lay beneath them.
When he made the father's rage explode across

a dozen angles or saved the drowning boy
with just a cut, the story saw him through.
In the next shot, a wrecking ball buckles

a brick wall. He plays it backwards, the sound
swallowed in reverse, then plays it again in slow
motion. He can't get over how the wall

keeps falling, like a man who tries to stand
again, then falls ashamed again, staggering
to his feet, only to fall once more.

AN OCEAN GLIMPSED THROUGH TREES

From my tousled bed, I wake to watch the world
turn toward light. A gray haze grips
the hills where grass sprigs poke through snow

that glows like the sea floor. Dawn's great
waters rise as our fishing boat
floats to harbor, its deck speckled with stars.

In an upstairs room, my young son shivers
in the half-light of moonlit snow.
If in his dreams the sea washes the land away,

nothing is changed. My love cannot save him
from the icy waters. And now sunlight strikes
the fluttering snowflakes. Our frail boat shines.

IN THE DARK MIRROR

Illogical this disappointment dogging me,
this loss and grief that weights my every step.
My children love me. My wife and I still laugh
and kiss. I have a house, a job, a car.

On a desert road, an old truck creeps through moonlight,
headlights off, its wooden sides stretched wide
by heaps of tires, hauled off for secret burning.

In the orange flare of gasoline-drenched rubber,
I am an ash cloud. I am a scorched field, dreaming
of green shoots. I blaze, then smolder in oily exhaustion.
The black smoke no one sees is choking me.

BENEATH THE SKIN

First I cut through skin and scales
just behind the gills.
When I set the knife aside,
organs dangle like a watch
of bone and blood sprung open.

I blindly took you
from waters where hidden paths
divide the weeds and rushes.
What did I look for
beneath your skin?

Strung across the city night,
a picture of a life
glows in each apartment window—
jewels sparkling
on each bone of your spine.

WITHOUT THE MOCKINGBIRD

Each day I work in a downtown
office, where spiky balls,
like porcupine quills, are mounted

along window ledges to prevent
pigeons from building their white
excrement-encrusted nests.

Sometimes, laid in an opening
where spikes have broken or bent,
I see their eggs, neither innocent

nor beautiful, but necessary to perpetuate
a waddling stiff-necked grandeur
among soot and shit and purple feathers,

high above sidewalks and cardboard beds
and office workers, neither innocent
nor beautiful, but necessary to perpetuate

the same fleeting grandeur—
all of which is not to dismiss
the soul's mystery in the material world.

DOG AS MASTER

Moonlight bathes the snowy hills
in a transcendental light, but she lives

for the stories beneath her nose,
the soap opera plots she sniffs out.

Yesterday's a forgotten bone,
how I hurried the mower back and forth

over plans and worries, until the acrid odor
of dog crap emptied my mind of tomorrow.

As I hosed it off the wheel,
she stared at me with quiet eyes.

Tonight, she dashes up the trail,
and never stops to wonder at stars,

but plunges her snout deep in the sloppy pocket
of the sensual present, her tags jingling

like thumb cymbals, her tail conducting
woodwind melodies of happiness.

LILACS

Van Gogh, 1887

Where brush encounters canvas
energy flows from bristle
to cloth, like God's finger

reaching down to make
Adam. Purple and white
blossoms jabbed on dark

green foliage pulse
with passion. Orange-red
strokes flicker in the foreground,

stabbed there by the stiff
bristles of a reckless brush.
Within them, the "V" of Vincent

is barely visible. He set
down his paints and stared
at a small rectangle bursting

with the beauty of agitation.
Even flowers tremble
with joy and anguish.

LEARNING ITALIAN

I am—pockets empty, mouth full of dust—the village idiot,
lips and tongue struggling to shape sounds
like a patient thick with Novocain, and eloquence
choked to stammering simplicities:
"my name is…," "it is beautiful," "goodbye."

But in the sound of words trickling
from my tongue, I taste my mother's homeland.
Il mare washes blue light and lapping waves.
Olivo and *aglio* glow like sun-drenched hillsides.
Pesce, pane and *vino* adorn the table in Vernazza,

where cobblestones lead to the tiny harbor
scattered with fishing boats painted
verde, marrone, azzuro, giallo, so the heart
will pull the nets each day, along with the hands.
Barco for boat, *cuore* for heart, *il barco del cuore*

skims the bright blue *mare, il mare azzuro,*
while on the hillsides, olive groves - *oliveto* -
surround the winding vines of the *vigneto.*
No wonder Dante rhymed the Commedia
and my mother smiled whenever she spoke Italian.

THE POET AND THE DANCER

When two such different people meet, muscles stretch.
She was his charley-horse; he was her shin-splint.
I knew them so well, they were like a quarrel
inside me. When he first saw her browsing the drugstore
shampoo, he thought he understood the jut
of her hip. Her verbs were strong and sure. And when
she stood on her toes and reached into her pocket
for a twenty, he knew her nouns were grounded in
the spinning earth.
                          She tuned her body's intuition,
strengthened it with sweat and pain. And when
she performed it was all her essence and somehow not
her. The first time he saw her dance, he felt
the burden of meaning lighten. He looked at the young
man lifting her and wondered why she didn't
sleep with him. She said: *if uttering that*
shortest word, "I," separates us, why not
desire something beyond us, and submit to love
or art or beauty?
                          They must have made love
in oppositions, eyes open, eyes shut, fueled by
longing, anxious to give. He would watch her surrender
to the coursing counterpoint, as if the bows
and fingers of a string quartet sounded all
her sixteen strings.

When he hid in his soul's dark
corners, she waved her hand to sweep away
the gloom. She said: *desire creates light—*
the white-hot laser of lust, the sputtering glow
of human love, God flashing codes across
dark seas.

She was the tree's leaves torn by wind,
not its hidden roots. Yet they shared the silence
of water rising from root to leaf to air.
Hand in hand they walked, one intent on translating
the world, the other intent on being it.

PEONIES

Tightly bound superball blossoms
burst into rippled petals
like a well-guarded secret let out.
The ants have done their magic.

And now the sheer brainy weight
of shaggy heads stoops each stalk
across the others—a rugby team,
arms embraced, falling down drunk.

KNOTTED ROPE

A bear sleeps in a cave of blue ice,
deep in my chest, where frozen streams lie
like unspoken words.

There is nothing to rouse him:
no dripping thaw, no April green
shouting from gray wilderness.

Even the rocks, carried within
the cold hand that carved these valleys,
have forgotten their journey.

At the cliff's edge a rope bridge,
swaying above the chasm, ties me
to a land, where people run laughing

as their skin shrivels to bark, their hair
becomes a vein of gold, their bones
go off to swim in oceans.

Rivulets of water etch the earth
around green gravestones —
red buds bursting

from limbs of stone,
a jungle springing up
as snow melts wildly away.

MEETING YOU

The wind tears the kite caught in the oak limb.
Distant lightning and the scent of rain,
as garbage cans crash and roll in the alley.

This can't be love, this three-stringed violin,
this house with no front door,
hearts scraping melodies with missing notes
and everything rushing in or rushing out.

Birds migrate by magnetic pole.
You bend the wind, throw the compass off,
lead the badger to rock-hard ground.

Wind-blown wrappers and newspapers
cling to the house. Rain flies against
my window, a thousand lost birds.

This can't be love, this black dog chasing its tail,
this boulder falling through still water,
a Texas tornado of fur and teeth
and the salt taste of your flushed cheek.

A Steady Light

SUN SWIRL WATER SILENCE

Goggles masked their eyes,
water slid off their sunlit shoulders
and the pool-swimming boys
were no longer boys, but animals sleek
as otters, intimate in their twisting shapes,
thriving in the distant country of childhood,
where the mourning dove sings
in solitude and the cottonwood seed
moves at the wind's pleasure.

Exhausted by light, we ride home,
as the long day's heat relents.
Does the woman I love see
the last red aura bathe the treetops?
Does our son linger in animal grace?
We travel in still worlds of thought and impulse,
though language can lift us, like otters' play,
out of isolation. I can just reach
to touch her shoulder, his knee.

TENDING THE FIRE

for Gabe and Jamie

Up at the lake, tending the fire
is all you wanted to do.
We burned dead wood
we had gathered,
crumpled the year's newspapers
and watched them curl into smoke.
As night fell and cool air
blew in off the lake,
you two made torches
out of twigs, and carrying
your small light walked
hand in hand away from me
into the dark, private places
you have always had.
Leave me as you must,
for minutes or years,
and I will keep this flame
bright enough
for you to rediscover
our common fire.

LOOK OUT THE WINDOW

As the car begins to slide beneath you,
snowbanks slowly twist on a giant spindle.
You pump the brake once or twice, then stop.

Plans for the day melt away.
In another slow rotation of the car,
it will be spring.

Look out the window.
Your children, suddenly grown,
do not have time to wonder

why you love to watch the moon
inch through branch and twig,
and quietly break free.

HOME PREGNANCY TEST

Not the mother whispering to her daughter that the flush
of her skin heralds a holy arrival, not the doctor
discovering the jarring fact in the course of a routine
exam, not angels fluttering, trumpets sounding,
and an epiphany fit for the miracle of another ordinary
savior—but the deep yellow wash of urine
over a plastic wick pungently announcing, yes
the sperm and egg have met, and are shacking up
in the same hovel where new love rules
and stacks of dishes go unwashed, sheets
unchanged, phone calls unanswered, library books
unreturned: they are blissful in their union and out of
the indolence of love comes the industry of building
cells for eyes, tongue, pancreas, ear lobes,
knuckles, and the stubborn soles of tiny feet.
Put away your bedclothes, put away the cardboard box
and instructions, climb into the slipcase of sheets
with me, for within you now, tinier than
your heart, your stomach, the grapes and pasta you ate
for dinner last night, is a new being, shaken
with rhythm as you practice your ballet leaps, busy
changing everything within your ballet spin.

BIRTHING GEORGE

For months your belly swelled, until you both
ran out of room—he moved under your skin
like a fish caught in a wool blanket.
It took hours to navigate your body, the narrow channel
stretched by his skull as your bones flexed. He turned
to clear the pelvic opening, then twisted between
pudendal and tail bone, his fear smothered within
your flesh, as you screamed and cried. Finally his head
appeared, his matted black hair and puffy
face between your legs—creature with a woman's
torso for his body, a woman's legs for arms.
Then the rest of his nakedness burst from yours,
and the umbilical cord writhed like a snake, winding
its way out of your insides to his very middle.
A slow waterfall of blood ran
from your body down the blue surgical drape.
He gasped, then cried—newborn testing air
and voice, weary traveler who finds himself
in an unexpected place. The doctor grasped
the cord that tethered his life to yours,
then clamped and cut the living rope
and his blood became his alone.

BY THE POND AT 5 P.M.

As my young son runs through reeds
and tosses twigs at ducks
that scurry, mutter and curse,
one by one commuters
guide their steel shells home.

Last night the flu kept me awake,
and this walk has drained my strength.
I drop the dog's leash, letting her
sniff and roam the shore, as the sun
melts my last lump of ambition.

Now I am an old man hunched
on a park bench, weary of striving,
weary of coveting things and glory,
filled with a sense of folly
that turns a man bitter or wise.

A man in suit and tie hurries home.
He chats on the phone, steers round
the bend and nods in my direction.
I straighten up and wave, and the electric
garage door yawns and swallows him.

NOTHING NEW UNDER THE SUN

Having seen go-go boots return to fashion,
Three Dog Night reprised from restaurant speakers
like an auditory Agent Orange, I'm not surprised
when the preacher shouts *there's nothing new
under the sun.* But George frowns.
Eight years old. The Lewis to my Clark.
Together we explore our ordinary
yard and revel in the moth's befuddled
flutter, the squirrel's chittering tail.
For him, the world's a kind of heaven —
the marvel of the dipping bobber, tiny
hook and soggy worm, the wonder of
who's nibbling below. The river he steps in
is always new. The hilltop view reveals
a virgin woods, a hidden falls, a species
yet to be discovered, or just a single
cloud plucked out of the day's parade,
to be claimed, pored over, named.

AWAY AT COLLEGE

She's sobbing, late at night, the telephone
a cold comfort, pressed to her ear and mine.

He's ruining my life, she says. Love
is such a bastard. Men are goats.

I left her mother just before her fifth birthday.
At her party, little girls played

while their mothers scowled at me.
This goat broke her mother's heart,

left a home with two children
to find that bastard, love.

Last leaves sail in wet autumn winds.
I turn on the heat. Pour a drink.

Love can save your life, I tell her,
as the furnace flame whooshes and the season turns.

THE QUIET

The phone rings as dawn's glimmers
gray the bedroom window. He's OK, he says,
then speaks slowly of the ambush,
the quiet before the trip wire, the bomb
that didn't explode, his jammed gun,
the man above him on the roof. He's OK,
OK. And I stare at pools of water
from the night's downpour, the soaked
earth, the swollen gullies,
the water's dark body
that seems to glow from within.

THE WATER TABLE

First day of spring. Sparrows flutter close to the ground.
Stopping for lunch in this highway blink of a town,
I slide my tray along the cafeteria rails,
where the homemade sign points
to a cup taped to the top of the cash register.
Collection for Joe Martinez whose son Eldon was killed in Iraq.

Not my son. Not this time, I tell myself.
But the ice sheet on the lake begins to sink.
Thin streams trickle away from black
mounds of snow in parking lots.
Aquifers collect dark water. Hidden caverns fill.
Wet leaves clog the thawing gullies,
as water runs under the earth.

SEPARATION

At eleven in the morning, darkness fell.
My son reached for my hand, but I was gone.
Like a sun-starved plant gone stringy

and bare, he struggled after that.
Strata of buried homework hidden
beneath books and backpack,

and a hollow spot within,
like the sunken circle in the yard
where once the elm tree rose.

In the newspaper: a mother
snuggles her children in their seats
before rolling the car into the lake.

Children can live under the water.
When they emerge on the far shore,
you cannot take your eyes off them.

One night I found him in the kitchen,
his muscular chest and skinny legs
covered in long underwear.

He was writing a song called "Eating
Mr. Hoover." At Mass next morning,
he pocketed the Eucharist.

The wafer of bread, the body of Christ
rested in the dark tomb of his pocket,
as if awaiting resurrection.

Each day I check the mailbox
for a small blue envelope, a soldier's
letter, words full of the distance

between Minnesota and Iraq.
He tells me stories of himself,
without the ending.

I can hear their rustling wings
at the door. When I open it,
long, feathered necks crane,

talons claw at his ID, his sad,
hard face. But there is no hand
to reach for or touch.

MIDDLE OF LIFE

1 The tree spreads slender shoots.
In the crowded forest,
some find light, some shadow.

2 In the morning, smoke rises
from the power plant in a still column—
by afternoon it's blown away as fast as it appears.

3 The stream swells and diminishes, carving
its earthen banks through the seasons, writing
and rewriting its many-syllabled name.

4 A rope leads from house to barn, guiding you
through the blizzard to feed the hungry livestock.
But somebody has moved the barn!

MY FATHER'S BLINDNESS

The front door squeaks in my father's house,
as he leaves for his morning walk.
A chattering in the treetops. Birds whistling
the sound of sunrise for the blind.

While he listens to lectures on Shakespeare,
never losing his stride,
I nestle closer to my sleeping wife.
Blackbirds wing from silhouetted trees.

I close my eyes and practice.
Scent of eucalyptus on the ocean breeze.
Scent of her hair. No shimmering or shine.
No wash of whitecaps to the shore.

We walk to the store and he doesn't want
my arm, feels his way around the aisles, finds
his favorite crackers, but now there are five
flavors, all the same size and weight.

The eyes send out their signals. Glances
brush against us like a sudden evening breeze.
Her eyes lock to mine and curtains open.
His pupils are gray and disconnected.

Wrack of sea scum, stones, rotting kelp
on the beach below. Raindrops dripping from
the gutters. Her smooth belly as she arches
her back. A fire on the shore.

My father washes up before the darkened mirror.
He never speaks of going blind.
Night falls in the sound of crashing waves.
We cannot look into each other's eyes.

A STEADY LIGHT

1.   *October 14*

For two days we have punched in and out,
sleepwalkers working the line, where God assembles
another death. By turns grieving or bored,
we chatter, fall silent, weep quietly, then one
by one step outside to feel the warm sun's
indifference. In other rooms, patients pick
at food or sleep beneath the TV's ghosts.
None of them seems so finished with life.
I kiss his forehead. He smells of death, this man
who carried me on his shoulders like an infant prince.

2.   *October 15*

Three days since the stroke. White hair,
white beard, face ever turned
skyward, he's a prophet defying the world,
these distracted ones seated in a circle
around his bed. Eyes closed in fierce
concentration, each heaving breath
lifts him away, so slowly we hardly see.

3.   *October 16*

Why can't I pray as my father lies dying?
I have no words for God, no plea.
Shouldn't this death, my death,
bow my head, bend my knees? Instead,
each gasp steals me from the God
I find I hardly know, and now refuse to seek.

4.   *October 17*

I did not see my father's ghost rise
from his still body, but I followed him into hunger,
a hunger for the siren song, the driftwood fire,
the cold journey into dawn, tangled
thighs, tender belly. She pulls me to
her pillow. I sink with a drowning man's
resolve. My body dissolves with the ship bell's
brass, the abandoned ring's gold.

5.   *October 18*

Yesterday your last breath passed.
Your stillness is complete. Your body cold.
In your garage, I find a baseball nestled
among the tools. I used to chase fly balls
you launched, making the running catch, then
whirling to throw the ball back. You never minded

that the throw went wild, skittered past the backstop,
as you tossed the next one up and whacked it.
The ball's long arc connected your
bat, my glove, a man's hands,
a boy's hands, touching through the white
flight across the cloud-strewn blue.

6.   *October 20*

The day of his funeral, a gray cloud rises
to the north, ash blows over the mountain
from a valley fire. Particles of trees and scrub
brush have seeped into the house and coat
the bookcase shelves, like the many parts
of him I never knew and now never will.

7.   *November 2*

I whispered in his ear because they said
he might be listening. I whispered, come back
to me when you are gone. Come back
so I can see that you are there, somewhere.
And now I watch. Maybe the curious wren
at the window. Maybe the squirrel, day after day,
eating the pumpkin on the stoop. But nothing really.
Until a sentence comes suddenly to mind,
as I wander downtown streets. Four sudden

words stop me. Let God love you.

8.   *November 12*

Traveling. The train rumbles through a dark
tunnel in Tuscany and I am Aeneas, man
without a country, on an underworld journey
to search among the shades for my father.
When the train bursts from shuttered rumbling
into green hills, windblown trees
and a plunging stream, I see what my father saw.
Out of days of labored breathing, he gave
birth to his death in a sudden rush of light,
not the light of afterlife, but this life,
not a new world, but this world—
thunderclouds and silhouetted olive
trees and mountains drenched in eerie rays—
an old world, magnified and lit
and seen all at once, every leaf
and stone, breath of wind, dewdrop.

9.   *November 22*

The first violinist pulls her hair back,
plucks each string, and turns off her cell phone.
The cellist puts aside his afternoon appointment
with the lawyer. Each player pauses before
the beetled darkness of Beethoven's last quartet.

Then, wind thrumming their taut sheets,
the four keels of a delicate armada are swept
along by the energy that carries us into death—
wooden ships flying through uncharted air.
When tremors fade from singing hulls, silence
deepens. Part of the mind still listens through Ludwig's
stone-deaf ears. The traveler returns from the stormy
rim, missing the one who crossed over.

10.   *December 14*

Twilight. 21 degrees. Winter silence
wrapped around me like a steel container.
Telephone wires scratch the sky in loops
and arcs. Leafless trees, completely still,
form a haze of veins in search of life.
Engines hum on the road across the barren
cornfields. Sometimes a glimmer of headlights,
like souls traveling close to the blanketed earth.
How does the soul know what to do,
where to go when the body dies?
Without its anchor in muscle, blood and bone,
does it wander, homeless as a windblown cardboard sign?
When will he come and speak to me, my dead
father? Is he still finding his way?
Or are his words the source of all these mysteries?

THROUGH THE VIEWFINDER

Say the son gathered seeds from palm
trees, and took them home to plant in pots
his mother used for marigolds and mint.
Down the hall, his sister starved herself.
Springtime came, and the son placed the seedlings
on the backyard deck. One night, his sister's anger
blazed, a fierce light that withered all
the family hothouse held. She woke her parents,
her slashed wrists bleeding on the white rug.

Say they took a family trip to Venice,
the father finding hope in the stolid grandeur
of homes that somehow rose from streets of water,
the mother watching the sure movements of men
who worked the transport boats, turning them
with a rudder twist and the engine slipped in reverse.
The son ate *sarde alla griglia,*
grill-blackened tiny fish. He tore
the backbones out, bristling with white gleanings,
then ate the tender, moist filets. Perhaps
they took a water taxi to San Michele.
Maybe the day was warm with Mediterranean
sun, but cooled by a breeze that blew from sea
to mainland. The cemetery island offered
lofty cypress trees and songs of hidden

birds, just what they had missed in Venice.

They walked together as a family, sometimes
holding hands. They admired the large stone
vaults with rows of square niches, like safe
deposit boxes. The daughter steered them toward
a row of crumbling graves, a children's row.
One gravestone held a metal frame,
a picture of a boy who died at eight.
He sat beside the street, smiling over
his shoulder, his dark eyes lighting up
the camera. His shaggy hair revealed his comfort
with eternity. They stared into his eyes
and saw the seed of death. Each felt
a sorrow, as fixed in everyday worry
as the daughter's crisscross of scars, each
of them alone, but linked, like the one long
ago, who must have set the camera down,
looked into his eyes and kissed his cheek.

MATTERS OF FAITH

While I listen to birds singing spring's
exuberance, my son fights a war in Iraq.
Men with rifles, bombs and grenades
want to kill him. And fearing for his life,
he questions every face he sees.
How long shall I cry and you will not hear?
Habakkuk demanded.
How did he know you cared to listen?

*

Making his first communion, my youngest son
swallows the body and blood of Christ,
a commingling of flesh that demands we look
through eyes of mercy and walk the trackless desert
with trust. Instead, I cling to grievances
and question every grain of sand.

My son says: God lives in the thoughts of people.
God has so many homes and can be in them all at once.
But if there were no people, would there be no God?

My son says: God loves us most of all creation,
but lives in other creatures too—maybe in their thoughts,
but maybe in their fur or skin or scales.

I think he loves animals because they're helpless,
they don't have guns or bombs. Once I cried
when I saw a crow eating a dead squirrel in the road.

*

The crow says: From the snowy branch
of the white pine, from my perch above
the bright hills, I stretch my wings and fall
into flight, seeking the gouge of mud among
mounds of melting snow. I sink talons into earth,
anticipating the day's carrion, for never have I seen
a day of life without death.

*

Looking into the faces of the men and women
gathered around the altar, I see their frailty.
We are brittle as pine cones, seeds released
by fire. We live in a dangerous world
whose fabric frays, and every surface cracks its glaze.

Fissures in the road reveal the stress
the blacktop cannot bridge. Wrinkles radiate
from the corners of my eyes. Deep below the sea,
molten rock erupts into water
from gashes in the earth's crust.

God becomes visible in the cracks,
the fiery lava churning beneath the skin,
and around these boiling vents creates
giant crabs and worms, feeling their way
without eyes, through cold, black waters.

*

The taxi takes us east of the Coliseum,
nosing its way between scooters and cars.
In the Chapel of St. Sylvester, where plaster
has fallen from the dim, dingy walls,
we pass from panel to panel, as Constantine,
disfigured from the plague, is blessed,
healed, and converted, in the iconic confluence
of story, feeling and light.
                                    Did the miracle
of healing deliver him to you? And through him
millions more? Who among them believes
without a glimpse of transformation?

*

When people are doing nothing, when they
are seated, waiting for the plane to take off,
their eyes look inward, a silence folds

the forehead and mouth, their faces fall
into grace.

        Confronted by grief, we row
across a roiling lake. What if I haven't had
my share of grief?

*

Let gutters ring with rain
running off the roof. Let beauty
fail. Let the day grow dark

with dread, as black cloths drape
the strangling sky. Like muddy hands
my garden gloves cling to earth.

Let beauty fail. Let despair wind
its way over every light, only
do not abandon me.

*

Pushing through snow puddles, a Mercedes
splashes water in low arcs, echoing the shape
of Michelangelo's Pietà, its form alive
in a muddy spray.

        Downtown, a yellow

crane hoists a beam atop another office tower.
In the streets below, there lives a child whose parents
forget him in drink, an old woman lost
in vivid memories in the nursing home,
a young man who goes to work, comes home,
and speaks to no one.
                    For each of them,
the yellow crane lifts a beam and sets it
where workers with rivets and torches
bond the bones of a new monument in the air.

Walking in the melting snow, what is my prayer?
The path of right-thinking leads to a still lake.
But who can save my son?
When the roadside bomb thunders—a dazzling flash
and steel shards shredding his Humvee—who
will raise him out of tar-black smoke
and set him on his feet beside the road?

SUPPOSE

Suppose that once lulled half asleep by heat
darkness and endless desert road   then shocked
awake by an explosion   heart pounding
brakes screeching   sudden bright flames
from the first truck   stutter of automatic weapons

suppose you decided to charge into the night
firing at flashes in the roadside ditch
shouting at the stifling heat   moving

calmly through flying metal then heaving
a grenade into the ditch reeds and feeling
after the blast the slap of swamp water
black rain of mud and slime then more

shouting and final nervous spurts of gunfire
before the sudden quiet drenched in smoke
and a tense inventory of loss in the stranding
darkness. Later in life, would you savor

the everyday, or find the ordinary moment
pale? Maybe a steely resolve, or haunted core.
I can only imagine, for you won't say.

When you returned, you stood in the grocery, staring
at green asparagus, red peppers, yellow
papaya.
Maybe imagination's greatest
trick is to let us move another's muscles, taste
another's pain. What grace shone in the leafy
greens and orange tangerines?

Three Women

THREE WOMEN
(and a Recurring Apparition)

East

Sometimes I count the sun's seven-hour swing
and wonder where you are—lying on a Calabrian
beach beneath the stunning Mediterranean sun,
or drinking with your friends. Once when you called
I heard their sing-song banter, Italian
broken by youthful laughter, and speeding past
my schoolbook learning. So the different paces
of youth and age make wildly different lives.

Here at home, I'm focused on a different facet
of age—the changing love of long marriage.
As you may someday see, romantic love
is not the love of the long-married, a variant
for centuries unnamed. For my parents,
it was sixty-seven years of harmony.
Such simple chords have never worked for me.
But what about you? You've escaped
your spa job, tepid boyfriend, years
of school. We're both keeping watch over
the bows of our ships. But while you're scanning
the skyline for new lands, I'm watching the water
ahead for rocks.

        Does the subject of love
make you wonder why I left your mother
those many years ago? Self-preservation,
the need to be in love and loved. Was that
indulgent? Too much self-love? I thought
a happier man could be a better father.
You and your brother survived divorce, new
marriage, loved the baby George, and we lived
in a golden age—fabulous (I think),
but brief. Too soon you left for school, your brother
left for war.

        Just weeks ago, the crickets
began their nightly song, with tree frogs
and katydids in counterpoint. Summer's
swarming life has peaked and now the light
crosses into autumnal blue, the brilliant
clarity of the great swoon. I pick tomatoes
from tangled green, slice and layer them
with mozzarella and basil, and taste the summer
bounty. I sit on the screened porch, safe
from touchy wasps, and delight in browned grass
that doesn't need mowing. In Minnesota,
you learn to love each season for its extreme.

South

In these days of falling, leaves skim and skitter
on autumn streets, the rabble of our lives,
evidence of our chaos. Maybe I'm too brittle,
and you too given to flash points of anger.
Together we have smoldered in the fields, piled
among abandoned cars, waving fitful
arms of smoke, never utterly consumed
until now. We turned our lust to love,
and fanned it into lust again. Love
and lust carried us past the hurtful words.

After fifteen years of marriage, we drift
from the plain wooden dock of our pledge.
Two children led us up the aisle, and you
so young yourself. You wore your mother's dress—
stitched white folds, pleats that traced your waist
and breasts, brocaded lilies clinging to
your innocence of all that followed. Months later,
shoveling the driveway, I looked up from moonlight-
drenched snow to yellow light spilling from
a window. Three faces of a new family watched me,
the one we made together still unconceived.

What do I love about you? Your passion,
impetuosity, the way you never fail
to challenge me, your wisdom in raising children,

your touch. But remember our trip to the North Shore?
We fought on the drive up, and when we arrived
gale winds hurled the water over itself,
wave after wave, as in long marriage
the glib satisfaction of being right thrashes
love. Our scraps of good intentions tumbled
away like broken stalks and driftwood shards.
All day, we did not speak.

                                  Never restless,
except when filtered by rustling aspen leaves,
never the turbulence of water, anger
of flame, eccentricity of air, light
saturates the world, warms my jean-clad legs
to bone. It lingers where absorbed, dances
where reflected, then climbs the treetops, and leaves
behind the unconstellated stars. Light
will lead me through this turmoil.

                                  You travel south
to your childhood home. The Mississippi flows
from here to there. I could send this letter
to you in a bottle, floating past the grain
elevators, pleasure boats and river barges,
but it would surely lose its way— just
a lost letter, drifting downstream, between
two people, bound in pledged union, and now
unable to find the will to speak.

West

So strange to think you're west, a westerner,
with views of mountains, sea and desert scrub,
a land like the one your parents left, voyaging
to Chicago's little Italy. But what would Grandpa
think of Santa Barbara, Oprah and the homeless?

As a child, I cringed when you served my friends pasta
in a walnut anchovy sauce. But I loved your love
of food, the wanton way you tossed the onion
in the oil, tested the pasta with your teeth,
and patrolled the table, wiping hands in apron,
as, prayers said, the family ate and passed,
ate and passed.
                The weather turned this week.
Ice thickened over the pond, and snow
fell last night. I woke to a shining world.
First snow fills my heart with hope. But the sparkles
that delight the eye come from the killing cold.
For like the ones you met with every childbirth,
all things are made of equal parts of pain
and glory.
           As winter whitens my view, rain
inspires the birds of paradise and bougainvillea
to bloom along your streets, where eucalyptus
trees sway above rust-free classic cars, eternal
forms that seem to mock their sun-worn drivers.

Thirty years ago you two trekked west
and seemed to join the timeless. So when the stroke
shut him in a coma, and days of labored breathing
followed, I didn't know what to do.
You touched his hands, stroked his hair, whispered
in his ear. Your grief was sometimes wide and calm,
sometimes raging, white and broken, a river
forced through narrows and sudden turns.
And with his startling silence, you somehow grew
stronger. I hope when I am ninety-one,
I watch movies, see friends, and still cook, like you.
The poster-size portrait for his funeral
provides the watchful eyes you need, as you sleep,
dress, read, and cheer the Lakers. Even now,
the steady-state condition of your marriage
remains a mystery. Never a thrown dish,
or even a raised voice. The other day
I passed an arguing couple on the street
and wondered if you two still share the happy
dissatisfactions of everyday life.

A good Italian mother, happiness
is what you want for us, to love ourselves
as you love us. Of all the types of love,
self-love is wayward, as you well know, and given
to bouts of self-pity, but its molten
core shapes us, and forms the volcanic soil

from which the forest grows. The landscapes I've seen
while driving west are mirrored within: the arid
badlands and rocky mountain needs, but also
miles of fields to plant and harvest, that even
in winter are dreaming of their wheat and corn,
their terraces that ring the hills, their valleys
too deep to till.

North

It's odd how in this age of reason, we've
dissected, classified and cataloged
everything but love. Love is still a mystery—
as, of course, are you. For though I think
I know you, I do not, no more than I know
the sudden snowflake wandering in this morning's
sleet and haze, that disappears in spring's
softening mud.

                You, Venus, with your youthful
beauty, shine everywhere around me. And as I age,
youth itself becomes a marvel, a joy, with a sure
allure that can border on obsession. Augustine
said this world's things are good, but a lesser good
than God himself. The troubadours transformed
desire for the distant lover to longing for
the hidden God. The Sufis made love to God
in poems. And so I tell myself lies
about my purpose, as if my distraction by
your beauty could bring me closer to God. But how
can eros be transformed to charity?

                      In my dream,
you took the shape of a young woman at the dry
cleaners. Tall, dark-eyed, almond-skinned,
she was the real flesh and blood you.
I came back week after week to see you. And once,
we took a walk and stared at the sea. Did you sense

the water's desire to move as an embodiment
of feeling, to carry the minerals of my mortal nature,
to echo the agitation of earth and moon
and wind? The glittering water liberates light,
as spring comes to raise me from the long burial
of winter.
                      Don't let me say seize the day.
For the gray Baltic of the backyard scrub still stands
in frozen waves of dirty snow. So many
things to mourn, but hardest is what's never
to be. There will be no new entanglement
of love. And so this letter rests unsent
to you, whose home is in the low northern
sky. Look this way and watch the green
begin to follow the river—the beauty of bare
branches leafing out in olive daubs.

South, 2

Since your trip last fall, I've come to see
the subtleties of glances. When glances fly
between two people, one often chooses
to look away. But when both choose to let
their glances meet, or, when in conversation,
eyes linger one extra beat, the thrill
of possibility sparks between the eyes.
But what comes next?

                        I'm caught between
desire for the dizzy rush I've felt before,
and the puzzlement of what we might become,
the mysterious next phase of the long-married.
Yesterday, I drove a Maserati.
I flew like a winged god across the summer
sky, speed and agility at just a nod.
Can we shift our engine and whir our wheels
again? Here's a poem I wrote called "I, Jove:"

        We all think of ourselves as gods, don't we?
        And those we love, whether from afar,
        or as we wake beside them in our beds,
        are mortals—loved for their transient beauty, while we,
        away from the mirror, are forever twenty-five.
        So, I, Jove, bewitched by your youthful brilliance,

Europa, go to seduce you, not in my
full splendor, but disguised as a snow-white bull.
I'll lure you into climbing on my back.
You'll feel my shoulder muscles, as we stroll
through fields of flowers, skirt the foamy water's
edge, and, when you grow too comfortable,
swim into the salty sea, where you can't
turn back. My method of seduction depends
on transformation. But the story doesn't end
with penetration. That's where Ovid's wrong.
For many years we've lived together—god
and mortal, beauty and ancient, royalty
from distant countries. Our children walk with clear
and radiant brows. And I will live forever.
Do I find a new Europa?

                                    Why love each other's
aches and pains and sagging jowls? Is marriage
the way we come to know our dark side, our
inability to live in selfless love?
This letter shines a light on mine. And now
that you're back, no need for envelope and stamp.
I'll leave it lying on the kitchen table,
where flowers droop around the blue vase,
the smell of toast sweetens the air, August's
tomatoes glisten in slices for sandwiches,
and shed petals paint the disheveled richness

of our lives. Maybe, after you read it,
we'll look into each other's eyes.

North, 2

Your charm has wrecked so many lives. Not mine,
I pray. But I scan the horizon for your glimmer,
the face you glow within, your lithe legs
in running shorts, golden wisps of hair
adorning your golden arms.

                              In Ovid, the trick
of metamorphosis aids seduction and revenge.
Transformed gods seduce mortals or bewitch
the willful as stones or trees or birds. This mortal
lover could win the goddess, if he could hide
his wrinkles, but keep the wit and charm of age.
But mortals can't transform. And should I manage
to deceive, like all the desperate lovers in Boccaccio's
tales, I'd face your wrath. For you could shrink me
to a bonsai, dumped on your November deck.

I'm writing a poem that grows with every season.
Each compass point holds a woman's strength,
but one of them is ghostly as Helen,
who animates the siege and battles, but only
appears once or twice, passing along
the parapets. Which woman holds the center
of my rambling? And are imagined lives best left
to words not deeds? Are some things better un-
embodied, left to be idea only?
In the sexuality of flowers,

the pistil and stamen never meet, except
through intermediaries—the hairy legs
of bumblebees and clumsy wings of moths.

When Polyphemus sings a song of love
to Galatea, the young sea nymph hides
and listens. Polyphemus is a Cyclops,
the one who will someday capture Ulysses
and then be blinded in his escape. When warned
that Ulysses will steal his eye, Polyphemus
laughs and says someone has seized it now.
He sings his praise of Galatea in gentle
metaphors. And then he sings his anger
at her hard heart that causes her to run
away from him. But best is when he sings
how his great ugliness is really beauty:
the tangled hair on every limb is like
a horse's mane, and his one eye is like
a shield and great as the sun. And so, blinded
by the one he loves, he forgets just who he is
and can no longer see himself.

West, 2

Do you remember my friend, Luis? He had
a heart attack. He didn't hear his wife's screams,
or feel the hands that brought him back. He saw
a light, warm and intense as the first spring afternoon
that chases winter. And though he says he's not
afraid of death, he seems to cling to all
this world's particulars.

                        These frigid days
are short, but bright, the sky heartless and bewitched.
I feel winter happiness at evening—
delight in the warm womb of the house. I sit
by the rosy reading light, transported by
A Midsummer Night's Dream in deep midwinter.
At night, I feel the pillows of grass beneath
the mixed-up lovers. They sleep among spells
and confusion, and I doze as moonlight bounces
on snowy hills, and glows behind the bedroom
curtains, like the magic light of a movie projector
that spools out dreams.

                    But I wake from the wild
possibility of dream to find a narrow road
hemmed in by overgrown woods, hardly
a fork in the road to choose. A friend told me
to think about the many meanings of *cell*—
prison, honeycomb, monastery,
battery. Restriction leads to transformation,

power, liberation. Though Dad was struck
by blindness, he found new ways of making honey
in each sparking neuron.

                              At his funeral,
people said Dad was a saint. They didn't
live with him. The ones we live beside seem better
sinners than saints. Once you told me the secret
to marriage is to know each other's sore spots
and let them go. Marriages survive on kindness.
So maybe long marriage is where eros
and charity finally meet. As for sainthood,
I don't think I can meet the standards
for good behavior, but some days I feel
amazingly alive—a kind of electric
peace, charged and attentive, composed.

East, 2

As you while away your time in Italy,
mooching on your friends, I'm wondering how
the rest of us can find the path to paradise.
Today I walked along the river road,
the leaves a new, limpid green. I gazed
across the valley, but trees hid the view
below, where the river crouched, deep within
the path it carved.
                        No wonder Dante began
his book by telling us his age. At mid-
life we begin to know our journey's course.
Just out of college, you're finding friends, a job,
independence. But you will carve a path,
choose your twists and turns. And certain serpentine
tracks will choose for you. For many years,
I've clung to the rocky paths of Purgatorio,
grateful to be above Inferno's suffering
and reluctant to explore the thin air of mystic
Paradiso. But now I see it's all
about the light. The Buddhists ask how we
can live in now instead of need. And living
in the light is Dante's way. His angels are creatures
who embody light, creatures whose wholeness brings
pleasure. So how do we join this wholeness?
Some people enter through generosity—
like the love that raises another's child as if

she is your own.

 But I've been shipwrecked on
an island. I've struggled in marriage, dragged the burden
of my aging, and flown in lofty fantasy. Think of
Prospero—another exile (and good Italian).
Through the magic of his art, he conjured people
from his past and fenced with shadows, until
he fought his way into forgiveness. He left
his island exile and regained his rightful place.
So whom must I forgive? Not only those
who've wronged me, but myself, for the neediness,
impatience, and unkind acts that exile me.
But here's the thing for you—you must live
like both Ariel and Caliban,
in your flighty immaterial nature,
as well as in its dense foundation.

 My love
and I once sat at a terrace table overlooking
Spoleto. As daylight grayed, swallows swooped
above us, and out over quiet rooftops.
Exhausted from our day of travel, we drank
a Montefalco red, ate grilled lamb chops,
and finished with ripe pears, cool beneath
the melted warmth of sheep milk's cheese. We stumbled
to our room, tucked into the enduring stone
of an old palazzo, and fell into a dead
sleep, a sleep where dreams could never strike
a spark. At dawn, a barking dog woke me,

and, as I drowsed, consciousness itself,
lodged in every inch of skin, was sweet.

AT THE SHORE

The water was so still that first afternoon,
humid silence weighed on us.
Hundreds of miles from home,

we were cautious in each other's presence.
That night, as we wandered the fog-
laced shore, winds picked up.

Whitecaps blossomed on the water.
Breakers reached the rocks below our bed.
But it was not the spectacle of rocks and spray

that returned us to each other,
nor the nourishing shapes of sky and water.
Perhaps it was the water's sound

washing through us—a sound
of patience and generosity,
that softness can caress away

the stubborn strength of these rocks
left on the shore
of our long life together.

TRAIN

As clouds move in
and the light of day
fails before
its time, I ask
if we are strong
enough to carry
the chaff and grain
of our lives across
this darkening prairie.
Yes, you say,
our love is a five-
mile train,
leaving the solitary
grandeur of grain
elevators, and hurrying
through the sound
of wheels clacking
tracks that run
side by side
towards a dawn
that promises
neither ease
nor unbroken gladness,
but the certainty
of returning light.

LET GO

The subject of work has seldom inspired poets,
writers and painters, unless you count the Soviet
social realists, forced to glorify
women on the canning line, men making steel.
But when you lose your job, there's more to say.
It's like the storm that sweeps through the middle of Lear—
the King goes mad, the Fool's in charge, and things
go topsy-turvy.
                    When birds are nursed to health,
we let them go. And letting go is what we do
when children leave to make their own mistakes.
Freed from my confinement, the credit cards
slither from my pockets, the face on my license fades,
my fingertips' swirling ridges smoothen,
like a glassy sea that strands sailors. Our work
defines us, and yet so often is indefinable.
I raised and spent money. I made the band
play the tune together, so the trumpets didn't
drown out the saxes, and the rhythm section swung.
Ellington I wasn't. But I formed a sweet ensemble
from distinctive voices.
                    In January's frozen
stillness, frigid temps day after day,
impenetrable earth beneath a foot
of snow, I start to freeze inside.

Long darkness. Heartless brightening. The dead
go unburied. To cure his father's despair,
Edgar leads the blind Gloucester to a rise
in a field and tells him he stands on the edge of the cliffs
of Dover. Gloucester leaps, swoons, and wakes
to wonder why a miracle has spared him. I close
my eyes and leap from the Washington Avenue bridge,
where Berryman waved goodbye. Will I wake up?
Is there more for me to say?

                        Sing, Muse, of Everything—
love and anger, palm trees and dust, Mingus,
Stravinsky, rain, photosynthesis,
work, dream, Dostoevsky, Issa,
loss, beginning, the moment empty of meaning,
and the moment pregnant with mystery. Start with these
of all I would say.

                   Suddenly the house is
quiet as a mountain top after the storm's
blown through. I strap on skis and swoosh downhill,
afraid of getting lost, alive with possibility,
falling down into the bright world.

WALKING INTO THE WIND

Like a rich man who's lost his fortune, and lies down
in the dirt, its green crest is crushed against
the scarred ground, its wind-tossed leaves now still.
The moist scent of earth emanates from
its roots. They dangle in the air, their tangled

darkness brought to light. Along the street
that skirts the park, neighbors drive to work.
They turn and stare, and I wonder what they see
in the fallen tree, in the lone man who's not
hurrying anywhere. The sound of shearing

earth and snapping roots seems to echo
from the still-standing trees. Few are called
to be uprooted, as I was—toppled and torn
from my fenced yard, and waiting for the scouring
singe of flame, my restless purpose.

HAPPINESS

In Dostoevsky, the dying man proclaims
that Columbus was happy not when he had discovered
America, but as he was discovering it.
I think of this as I walk the dog, and birds
sing in the gloom, anticipating light.
The dog is from the shelter, and can't stand
to be out of my sight. She's glad I lost my job.
Reinventing myself and this worried dog—
that's the work before me.
                              We climb the summit
of these suburban hills, and strain to see
beyond the new circling road that strings
together gaudy houses, like baubles on a strand
of costume jewelry. The view behind I know—
the shooting stars of love, marriage, children,
jobs. But as for what I might become,
the distance is foreshortened, like a painting
without perspective.
                              When I was twenty-two,
I wandered the streets of Berlin, done with college,
no girlfriend. All up and down the Kurfürstendamm,
hookers stood in mini-skirts and fur coats
against the December cold. I took a train
to the Gemäldegalerie and found myself
eye to eye with a young woman in a painting,

attracted by her golden hair, the luster
of translucent brushstrokes that made her radiant skin.
Over her shoulder was a city on a hill,
its flatness unsettling, its materiality
untethered. The house of my new life shined
within its walls. This crazy vision of my future
filled me with the joy of one who walks away
from everything to gain everything.
This is how the spirit struggles to be,
appearing anywhere and anytime,
as then, a sudden apparition of meaning
over a young woman's shoulder, the one
I loved who could not see me.

                                  Happiness
is not the voltage surge that floods the brain
in bursts—the special purchase, love's spark.
It's a steady current charging limbs and brain,
a constant hum along the passageways,
like a child absorbed in thought and play, and humming
all the while, or the maker of things, who's open
to stumbling into what comes next. When turmoil
and flux overwhelm me, the only peace I want
is the pins and needles trance that's fully awake.
The daily bread I pray for is a firm place
to stand, from which to paint the clouds and hills.

EXPLORERS

It's been two years and where are you?
I stand at the shore of this lake you loved, trying
to sense your spirit, trying to leave the house
of doubt. I turn to you, my elusive father,
because you lost the sunlight glittering on the lake,
the long shadows moonlight draws from the ash trees.
Late in life, you felt your way through blindness,
and walked without fear.
                                        And late in life,
I've left my job with no sense of what comes next,
as people make a pilgrimage because
there's something they must see—the steps Christ
climbed to Pontius Pilate, the Buddha's place
of Enlightenment. I've set out to see
who I will be and what I'm capable
of discovering, an exercise of will, while uttering
thy will be done.
                            But is an explorer who's
uncertain what he hopes to find merely
a wanderer? Explorers often venture
from known to unknown, and mapmakers rely
on the restless. But no Everest looms
at my horizon. My charts and compass
lead me inward. And as my words explore
the virgin coast, its mist-soaked coves and capes,

I study the maps of storytellers, who've charted
the characters I know—conquistadors and searchers,
innocents, and lost dogs. Magellan sailed
mysterious seas, Peary trekked the arctic,
and Shakespeare dove into the madness of
the king who lives within.

                            When you and I
carried our canoe to this lake, I loved to watch
the water washing in and out, how
it floated bits of driftwood and broken shells,
until a stronger swell lifted them
further up the shore, into the grip of sand
and rock. And as we paddled out, buoyed by
the water, I knew the lake would not lift
those bits of shell and driftwood for hours or days.
But sometime in a storm, they would be swept
from shore again. I don't know what to pray for,
or if God hears my prayers. But I know
a story has begun.

THE GREAT LAKE

I row my boat beyond the river's mouth,
its creaking gunwales echoing from a cliff,
where an old spruce clings in dawn's half-light,
its gnarled roots like fingers folded in sorrow.

The thousand-foot dock, loaded with railroad cars
and iron ore, levitates over the lake,
a red-headed beauty dreaming beside the long
ship. Shoreline aspen glow like filaments.

Restlessly the water washes, rustling gravel
words along the shore, hiding drowned
sailors beneath its waves. The hull-held ore
glides away in silence to be transformed
by fire in the east, a blast furnace far

from grassy hillsides shining now with dew,
this just-born world struggling to its feet,
while I bend and pull these burnished oars,
handled by so many, words reaching
down again to stir this deep lake.

HEAVEN AND DESPAIR

I've never understood tears
of happiness, but I know heaven
and despair touch like dew and fog,
vapor to liquid,
liquid back to vapor. Aimless,

I drift among the willows,
a blue haze. I empty myself
into muscle, bone and sentience, a sudden
materializing
around a particle of dust.

I cling to a leaf and become
the cool wetness of well-being.
I turn lost into searching,
uncertainty
into deeply alive. Loss

prunes me back to trunk and roots,
teaches branches to reach for nothing.
Unashamed, I walk among
the prosperous,
seeker of mud, pursuing all

the appetites of love, praying
"Thy kingdom come" and knowing,
even as I scatter into worry,
fear, despair,
I am to touch heaven here.

FOR LOUIS, AT THE MEMORY CARE RESIDENCE

While the present dims, the past
grows bright, and you follow it
on a long walk through the woods

where the path slowly disappears
and the way back would be lost,
if you remembered having begun.

Looking into a still pond,
you talk to an old man. He laughs
with you, cries with your tears,

living his life again, through every
expression of your young face.
After years working the family farm

and jawing with neighbors at the bar,
you whisper beside the mirror
with the last one you love.

SOPRANO IN A BAKERY

Her feet grow tired of standing at her work
all night and so she hovers in her song, floats
among the ovens and trays.

Her voice, filled with the penetrating sadness
of a mourning dove, mingles with the scent of melting
blueberry, lemon, raspberry,

as she sings how she is waiting for something to happen
in her life. I want to go to her, touch
her long hair tied back

like a dream walker, but I have no part to sing.
I am the gray ghost she does not see.
We're like the father and daughter

in Ozu's *Late Spring*, she caught in the melancholy
of youth's encumbrance with doing, while aging requires
a restless questioning

of who I am, and no retreat into what
I hope to do. The night sky leans
over her solitude, crisp

points of light I cannot equate to a million
billion blazing suns. And how can the heavens
flame with boundless energy,

and here on this tiny planet so much torpor
and dinginess? Or maybe she sings beneath
a ceiling of stage glitter,

her blue eyes the color of sky that hides
the stars, her golden hair the color of light
that floods the sky. She

is all daytime and nothing of night. Beneath
her clothes she is the whiteness of the dough she kneads,
made from the stuff

of stars, creature of the bright night, sailing
among the fiery galaxies and struggling
to be awake.

BEAUTY WILL SAVE THE WORLD

Is it true, Prince, that you once said: 'It is beauty that will save the world'?

Dostoevsky, <u>The Idiot</u>

When my mother was inexorably
sliding toward her death—
trips in and out of the hospital,
days in rehabilitation
after her fall, the swift
decline of her mental sharpness—
I was swept up in confusion,
tasks and endless worry.

From the day she died onward,
I found myself staring
at murals on buildings, distracted
by the shimmering leaves of quaking
aspen, searching for music
of depth and shapeliness
on the radio. Beauty was a thief
bent on stealing me
from loneliness and grief. In color,
form and melody, I found
hope. A hidden brook
murmured of rocks that ripple
its glistening skin. Its touch

was cool and wet.

I waded in. I bathed
in the evidence of love.
I said to myself, look what
has been provided to you.

THE OLD BRIDGE

after Max Pechstein "Alte Brücke" c. 1910-1911

The old bridge arches across
the blue-green river, where ink-
black fish swim like a string

of dark, dreamless days.
When we close our eyes,
we're carried to the other side—

a garish fantasy
of pink clouds, orange
roofs and purple paths. Sleep-

walkers, we shrug our shoulders
against the day and fill
our silver pails until

they gleam with dream water.
When night falls, we
are free

as spread-armed shirts pinned
to a moonbeam.
We dance in a delirious wind.

THE LONG MELODY

for Gabe, Jamie and George

This heavenly city, while it sojourns on earth, calls citizens out of all nations and gathers together a society of pilgrims.
Augustine, The City of God

The weary man dozes, slips
from the sun's grip and yields
to the hidden moon.

A jellyfish floats beneath his mask.
Fish dart among anemones
and coral. But without his glasses,

the fish are yellow daisies,
blue lilies, the jellyfish
a rain-soaked newspaper.

He is a teenager, eating ice cream
at midnight. He swirls it in the bowl,
as her silk skirt swirled on the stage.

She waits for the arpeggios to rise,
poised among the bell choir's ringers.
Cradling the G and B flat,

she fixes her attention on the notes,
the conductor's eyes, the two bells
she knows are truth and love.

Just off the shore, a rock is submerged
by waves, then lifts itself through a veil
of froth as the current rushes out.

He stirs, and sees his children
shaping walls of sand, battlements that,
like their bodies, are fragile as

moth wings. They dig moats beside
feather-topped towers, straining
to hear him over the crashing surf,

but even in the quietest room
they listen to him with all their being
and one ear closed.

A whirling in air, wings
soaring, a feather-light,
sky-tumbling ecstasy

of flight, a living in air
and breath and nothing more,
a lightning bolt of likeness.

Look at the swallows, he says,
as he stares at the looping spires
of a blue castle, all its bells ringing.

AGING EYES

In the wrinkles of my eyes, I see my vanished days—
a life spent looking ahead to what I want to do.
If the blue jay lives in contemplation of time,
his sharp black eyes do not show it.

I remember staring at my father's weary eyes,
the sagging lids of many years. And now
my young son looks at me and sees the same.
But gazing at him, wild and precocious,
I see heaven's light. My eyes are wrinkled
but they know what they see.

Han Shan says, "Though face and form alter
with the years, I hold fast to the pearl of the mind."
Hidden within the shell, a part of me grows
more beautiful with time. The mind, round
and luminous, shines through aging eyes.

Many years I've climbed, feeling my way
through fog and mist. But when I live
in the empty cave filled with light,
I am free of cares.
Stepping sure, I walk on rock and cloud.

ACKNOWLEDGMENTS

These poems appeared in the following publications, sometimes in altered form or under different title.

Askew: Away at College

Atlanta Review: The Great Lake

Black Moon: Meeting You

The Bitter Oleander: Beneath the Skin

California Quarterly: Nothing New Under the Sun

Heartlands Today: Tending the Fire

Miramar: Aging Eyes; Happiness *(forthcoming)*

Nimrod International Journal: Separation

North Coast Review: Knotted Rope

Poetry Ireland Review: Home Pregnancy Test; Birthing George

Southern Poetry Review: Ice Storm

To Give Life a Shape: Poems Inspired by the Santa Barbara Museum of Art: The Old Bridge

Turtle Quarterly: An Ocean Glimpsed Through Trees

The Windhorse Review: Look Out the Window

FURTHER ACKNOWLEDGMENTS

I am very grateful for the many teachers, mentors and fellow poets who have worked with me along the way. I am especially grateful to Ron Starbuck for his expert guidance in the development of this book.

The following friends and mentors have provided helpful critiques and kind support and encouragement: Jeanne Murray Walker, Pete Fairchild, Greg Wolfe, Paul Mariani, Skip Renker, Thomas R. Smith, Mike Hazard, Jude Nutter, Ron Alexander, Enid Osborn, and Paul Willis.

Finally, I would be lost without the love and support of my family—my wife, Ellie, and my children Gabe, Jamie and George. And I am ever grateful to my incredible parents, George and Evelyn Thomas, who modeled for me the way to live a good life.

ABOUT THE AUTHOR

Daniel Thomas was born and raised in Minneapolis, Minnesota. He has published poems in many journals, including Southern Poetry Review, Nimrod, Poetry Ireland Review, The Bitter Oleander, Atlanta Review, and many others. He has an MFA in poetry from Seattle Pacific University. As an undergraduate at the University of Minnesota, he studied music, English literature and German literature. He then went on to study film history, theory and criticism at the University of Wisconsin, Madison and graduated with an MA.

His graduate degree in film led him to Twin Cities Public Television, where he was the video editor of an Emmy Award-winning national PBS series and producer of local documentaries. He went on to become COO of the PBS station. His long career in nonprofit management includes work as an executive director and a chief development officer.

In addition to writing poetry, he plays the guitar and writes music. For six years he served as vice-chair of the American Composers Forum. Dan is the father of three grown children. He and his wife, Ellie, moved to Santa Barbara, California in 2015.